Photograph...
Colin Je...

Front cover pa...
Julie Sto...

*We would like to thank the following for
permission to photograph their stock:*
**Hansards Pet Centre, Romsey
Kevin Curtis**

Your First
Ferret

CONTENTS

©1996
by Kingdom
Books
PO7 6AR
ENGLAND

your first ferret

Kingdom Books is an imprint of T.F.H. Publications   Printed in England.

INTRODUCTION

The ferret has been kept in captivity for centuries. In days gone by, wealthy people owned the hounds used to hunt deer, boar and other game. The ferret became the poor man's hound. It was easily housed and could be used on common land. Together with lurcher dogs, the ferret was kept by poachers, who ventured onto the estates of the rich to catch a few rabbits. Thus, the ferret became strongly associated with working people.

The ferret's reputation is rather unsavoury. It is credited with being savage, smelly, bad-tempered and untrustworthy. Nothing could be further from the truth. A ferret can be docile, friendly and entertaining as long as it is handled correctly from an early age. A ferret is not a suitable pet for a household with young children. It is not as mild-tempered as a dog or cat and will bite if handled badly. However, an older child familiar with handling animals can learn a lot about responsibility as a ferret owner.

The correct name for a female is a jill, and the male is called a hob. Baby ferrets are called kits.

Like many other animals, ferrets suffer at the hands of inexperienced owners. This book gives potential ferret owners a clear understanding of what they can and cannot expect of the ferret. A ferret is no more suited to

A baby ferret, about 12 weeks old, enjoys exploring its environment.

all people than are dogs or cats. A ferret cannot be trained like a dog, nor can it be given the outdoor freedom of a cat. However, if you are looking for a more unusual pet, yet one which does not demand a complicated diet or a great deal of maintenance, the ferret may be for you. A ferret can be kept safely with dogs and cats, provided that there is a properly supervised period of introduction.

Today, ferrets are enjoying a new popularity and many are found as pets in homes. As the ferret shrugs off its old negative image, it is seen in its true light.

HISTORY

The ferret is the domesticated form of the European polecat, *Mustela putorius*. Mustela is Latin for weasel; putorius is from the Latin verb *putor*, to smell bad. This relates to the fact that polecats have scent glands from which they release a foul-smelling liquid as part of their defense mechanism. There is still debate as to which wild polecat is the ferret's ancestor. *Mustela putorius* is considered the most likely, with the Russian species *Mustela eversmanni* as second choice.

The ferret belongs to the large order of animals known as **Carnivora**. The animals of this order range in size from the tiny dwarf weasel through to the largest land carnivore, the Kodiak bear. Between these extremes are many familiar species: lions, tigers, dogs, cats, seals and walruses. Although principally meat eaters, most carnivores are also secondary vegetarians, eating grasses, berries and fruits. A few, like the giant panda, are exclusively vegetarian.

Based on their similarities to a supposed common plan, or archetype, the carnivores are divided into a number of families. These include **Ursidae** (bears), **Canidae**

A sandy-silver mitt.

(wolves and dogs) and **Felidae** (cats). The ferret is included in **Mustelidae**. This family contains animals such as otters, badgers, skunks, weasels, martins, wolverines, minks and ermines.

The mustelids are quite old. They were among the first mammalian types that appeared following the sudden disappearance of the dinosaurs during the Cretacecous period. Most modern carnivores emerged during the next period, the Tertiary (also known as the Age of Mammals). It is generally thought that the earliest carnivores of our times evolved from small animals like the civets, which today are regarded as living fossils. Civets are of the family **Viverridae**. They are similar to weasels in their general shape which creates some confusion when tracing the history of the domestic ferret. It is probable that references citing weasels used to hunt snakes actually describe the mongoose, a viverrid.

Many people think of the ferret as an all-white animal. This is because the albino is one of the most popular forms. However, ferrets can be bought in a variety of colours ranging from white to almost black. Indeed, colour breeding is a strong reason why some people enter the hobby. There is no doubt that colour forms have great appeal to pet owners, and much expansion is expected in this area.

A polecat silver mitt baby, about 12 weeks old.

Coloured ferrets settling down for a sleep in the sun.

HOUSING

A tame, well-acclimatised ferret can spend most of its time indoors at liberty. Even so, ferret keepers often provide a commercially bought cage or insulated box so their pets can take refuge in the evening. Pet shops offer a variety of durable, portable, easy-care cages for this purpose. All accommodation should be ready and waiting for the new residents, including an exercise pen, outdoor home, catchbox, and so on.

HOME ACCOMMODATION

Ferrets kept indoors require very little in the way of housing. Essential items are a cosy box or cage with a warm lining in which the ferret can sleep, a litter tray and food and water dishes. Owners with ample indoor space can construct an all-wire pen complete with a nesting compartment and play area. This pen can be placed outdoors during warm weather.

EXERCISE PENS

The ferret kept indoors will benefit from the time it spends in an outdoor exercise pen. A ferret enjoys short periods dozing in the sunshine but can suffer from heatstroke, so the pen must take account of these two factors. An outdoor pen should be as large as space and funds permit. A rectangular pen is better than a square pen of the same area, since the ferret is able to run further along the length. Essentially, the run is a box shape made of welded wire.

For two ferrets, a good length is 4.5 x 1.2 x 1m. Construct three wooden frames to form the sides and top of the

run. The timber should be solid, about 5 x 5cm or 5 x 2.5cm. Smaller frames are needed at either end, or they can be of solid timber 1.25cm thick. Cover the frames with welded wire of 2.5 x 2.5cm hole dimensions and of strong gauge (at least 19G).

Bolt the frames together on their top edges. Then bolt the bottom edge onto a concrete slab floor or into a solid concrete floor. The bottom edges can also be given rigidity with wooden or metal cross members. An access hole for your ferret - a pophole - in one of the end pieces also makes assembly easier.

A unit easier to move around can be assembled by using shorter frames, about 2m. If the pen is not to stand on concrete, then a fourth frame can act as a base. In this case, the unit can rest on lawn or bare earth. This basic unit can be modified to suit your particular needs.

For ease of access, the roof or a side panel can be hinged. If the unit contains a pophole, a simple slide-up shutter can be attached to close the pophole as desired. A shelter can be bolted on to the pophole as a refuge in which the ferrets can sleep or avoid direct sun. It must be made of good, solid timber to provide insulation. The roof should be hinged.

A mini playland can be arranged within the pen, comprising pipes, stacked logs, stones, a shallow pond and so on. The ferrets will amuse themselves for hours on end.

An even larger unit provides more scope, while a smaller unit is better than none at all. Such a unit can be unbolted if it needs to be moved, or can be made into a permanent pen. It is also possible to fit similar pens to your home. Simply install a cat-flap and the ferrets can come and go as they please.

OUTDOOR FERRET HOME

If your ferrets' home is to be outside it is essential that it is dry, away from draughts and constructed of easily cleaned timber. It should be as big as possible. If these requirements cannot be met, do not keep ferrets permanently outdoors.

A good ferret home is made up of three areas: a sleeping area, an exercise area and a toilet area. Feeding is normally done in the exercise area. Ferrets defecate at the place furthest from their sleeping area.

Above: A coloured ferret in an outdoor pen looks up towards the camera; its companion is asleep.
Below: Ferrets with a selection of toys and playthings that will keep them occupied.

To avoid underfloor dampness and wood rot, construct the home on wooden leg supports. This also makes routine cleaning easier because you do not have to bend down. The minimum dimensions required for two ferrets are 1.5 x 0.5 x 0.6m.

Make the sides and top using 1.25cm thick tongue and grooved wood or chipboard. A thickness of 2cm is better for the base, as it will be less prone to warping. Coat the inner surfaces with a gloss paint or emulsion impregnated with a pesticide. This discourages lice, fleas and other parasites from hiding in the crevices. The outside can be either painted or the wood treated with a coloured wood preservative. Extend the roof beyond the sides for an overhang. Cover this with a roofing felt to make it waterproof. Give the floor several coats of paint to prevent staining and smelling from urine.

You can make cleaning the toilet area really simple by cutting a hole in a corner of the floor. Cover it with welded wire mesh of 1.25cm hole size. Below this, fit a sliding drawer filled with sawdust. The faeces fall through the mesh into the drawer and the area is easily cleaned and freshened.

The internal layout of the home should consist of a sleeping area at one end, the play area in the middle and the toilet at the other end. Each area should be separated by a solid wooden wall. Make holes just large enough for a ferret to climb through. Alternatively, sliding partitions can be made.

Fit the two end rooms with externally opening solid doors to make cleaning easier. The exercise area should have a wooden-framed, welded wire mesh front. The mesh should be of stout gauge with 2.5cm hole size. This front can be hinged, though a totally removable door is easier for cleaning. A sliding shutter incorporated into the sleeping compartment, operated from the outside, allows you to shut the ferrets in one area while you are cleaning another.

FLOOR COVERING

Wood shavings, straw and hay make suitable bedding material in the outdoor ferret home. The idea is to provide a material to soak up urine and moist faeces. Use sawdust and wood shavings in the play area and toilet, and straw and hay in the sleeping area. Make sure that any wood product you use has not been chemically treated. Pine and other fragrant woods are best for controlling odour.

Straw should be clean and relatively dust free as too much dust can cause eye problems. Hay is fine in moderation but during hot weather, it can cause sweat rashes. Ferrets use dried leaves to make bedding nests and you can also use shredded and granulated paper available from most pet shops. Do not use newspaper as the printing ink is toxic and can cause stomach upsets. Avoid stringy packing material such as that used for china and glassware. These strands have sharp edges that can easily cut a ferret.

CATCHBOX

A useful extra on a ferret home is a catchbox which is simply a small box fitted to the back of the home. It is large enough for one ferret to climb inside through an entry hole. The hole is opened and closed using an external shutter. The catchbox can be solid wood with a plexiglass or solid lid. The front is welded wire. The catchbox allows you to lift out an individual ferret easily. The ferret can be enticed into the box with a tasty titbit.

RAIN COVER

Another useful extra for a ferret home is a clear sheet of plexiglass 12mm thick. Drill holes in its corners and hang it over the front of the home during periods of driving rain or snow. It should not extend the full height of the mesh so that it will not become soaked with condensation. Take it as high as the point which is protected by the overhang of the roof. It can be held in place at its bottom edge with simple butterfly swivel catches.

SITE

The site for the ferret home is important. Place it where your ferret can enjoy the early morning sun, yet still have protection from the elements; near a wall or under an overhang is ideal.

CLEANING

You must clean the accommodation regularly. The minimum is once a week but you have to clean smaller cages more often. You can use a mild disinfectant but be sure the home is dry before replacing the ferrets after cleaning. Change the bedding regularly and clean the food and water dishes every day.

THE PET FERRET

Before you buy a ferret, it is important to discuss the issue with the entire family. Everyone must be happy with the new additon to the household. A ferret certainly is not noisy; it is playful, even mischievous. It can be house trained in the same way as a cat. Its feeding routine is simple. And, as an extra bonus, any mice in the home will soon be gone!

This ferret is enjoying its bath, but its owner is careful not to get soap into its eyes or ears.

A ferret can get along very well with a dog or cat as long as they are introduced properly. About the only drawback is that a ferret cannot be allowed to roam loose outdoors. You will never see it again.

Ferrets are hoarders. This means that your pet may take an article and hide it in an unusual spot. Ferrets are also 'nappers'. They curl up anywhere to take a snooze, from the cupboard to your bed. Since a ferret is so lithe, it can get itself into all sorts of situations so, if your pet is not in sight, check open cupboards and drawers, or your ferret may be shut in for many hours.

Your ferret may curl up in your lap for some stroking. You might even be able to take it for a walk on a leash and harness.

TEMPERAMENT

Like any other animal, some ferrets are very placid and really enjoy handling and some are more temperamental. The important thing is not to mishandle a pet. Generally, a ferret treated well and handled often from a young age is quite tame. Problems occur only if the ferret is treated roughly.

AGE TO BUY

The younger the ferret the better, providing it has been weaned, so the ideal age is about eight weeks. If possible, choose one from a litter which has been handled regularly by its breeder. There is no shortage of ferrets, so there is no reason to consider an older animal.

Observe a number of ferrets before committing yourself to one. Find out if there is a local ferret club and attend a meeting. Ferret owners will be happy to talk about the joys and responsibilities of ferrets. A member may have a pet with a litter due or available. Visit the breeder and check the living conditions. The ferret accommodation should be clean and the breeder should be knowledgeable and confident.

Make sure your ferret is healthy. Look for round, clear eyes with no sign of staining or discharge around them or the nose. The nose is moist but not runny. The ferret's body is lithe and the fur is smooth to the touch, lying close to the body. If you brush the fur against its lie, it springs back to its normal position. There should be no sores or signs of parasites.

Like a dog, a ferret can suffer from distemper, so ask the seller if your prospective pet has received a vaccination against this disease.

TOYS

There is no problem finding toys to amuse a ferret. Balls dangling from string, bones, cardboard boxes, bits of wood and tubes to scamper through are all good ferret playthings. Be careful about supplying items that your pet could tear apart and swallow. A digestive blockage could be serious trouble.

GROOMING AND BATHING

Ferrets are extremely clean animals and, under normal conditions, do not require extensive grooming. Some ferrets do not like being groomed but others enjoy the feel of a soft hair brush on their backs.

If your pet should soil itself, sprinkle cornflour, talcum powder or chalk powder into the coat, then gently brush it out. A wipe with a silk scarf or chamois leather cloth adds a nice sheen to the fur. Baths can be given occasionally.

HANDLING

To lift a ferret properly, place one hand over its shoulders. Your thumb should pass under the elbow of one leg while the second finger passes under the other. Place your index finger under the ferret's chin. This hold supports the ferret's body without the need to support its rear legs. However, when lifting a pregnant female, always support her rear legs with your free hand. Always talk to your pet when lifting it. Approach it from the front so that it is not taken by surprise, as a startled pet is more likely to bite.

This is the correct way to hold your pet; it is virtually impossible for the ferret to bite you.

THE WORKING FERRET

There are as many, if not more, ferrets kept as working animals as there are kept as pets. First, I would like to correct some of the misunderstanding concerning ferreting. Some people argue that it is cruel to hunt rabbits using ferrets. It is not the ferreter's aim to wipe out the rabbit population but merely control it. The rabbit is driven out of its burrow by the smell of the ferret and into a net where it is killed by the ferreter. It is not the ferret's job to kill the rabbit. A rabbit is a clever and cunning animal; if it is young and healthy it has a very good chance of escaping from a natural predator. It can be argued that other methods, such as snaring or myxomatosis, are much crueller ways for the rabbit to die.

Your ferret does not have to be half starved and vicious to hunt. On the contrary, you need to know that your ferret will not bite you when you reach into the undergrowth to retrieve it, and it needs to trust you or it will not come out of the ground. Do not think that your ferret will become vicious if you use it to hunt rabbits; it will not, but will remain your friendly, playful pet. Make sure you go ferreting with an experienced ferreter who will teach you how to kill a rabbit quickly and humanely once it is in the net.

Ferrets are also used when shooting rabbits. Nets are not put over the rabbits' holes, so the rabbits bolt out across the field whereupon they are shot. Falconers use ferrets in a similar way, the difference being that when the rabbits bolt a bird of prey is released to catch them.

If you go ferreting, you will need to buy a locator collar and receiver so that you can find your ferret if it gets lost in the warren. You will also need a spade, purse nets, a carrying box, a knife and, of course, your ferret.

You must have permission from the owner before you go ferreting any piece of land, otherwise you will be breaking the law.

OTHER FERRET ACTIVITIES

There are many ferret clubs in Great Britain and you can find addresses from your local library, pet shops, etc. If you join a club you will get to know and make friends with other ferret keepers and can exchange views on keeping and breeding your ferret. Also you can show your ferrets in one of the different colour variety classes at the ferret club shows. Ferrets are also raced; this is done by means of a row of plastic drain pipes about six metres long laid on the ground. Ferrets are put in one end and the first one to reach the other end wins.

Above: Enjoying a drink at the garden pond.
Below: Ferrets, like this polecat silver mit, love to explore.

Commercially prepared ferret food is available from pet shops and should form the bulk of your ferret's diet, supplemented with canned cat food. Don't scrimp when it comes to selecting your ferret's food. The little bit of extra money that you may have to spend will ensure that your pet gets high-quality food that satisfies its nutritional requirements. There is no need constantly to change your pet's diet. This does not mean, however, that the diet should lack variety. Your ferret will enjoy sampling various kinds of titbits from your table.

MEAT

Some ferret hobbyists offer their pet meat scraps occasionally. If you feed your ferret meat, always make sure that it is fresh. The meat must come from a reliable source, such as your family butcher, and it must be as fresh as possible.

FISH

Most ferrets enjoy a meal of fish, which you can offer as an occasional variation to the regular menu. Choose a non-oily fish such as trout or flounder, and make sure it is de-boned and fully cooked.

VEGETABLES, FRUIT AND CEREAL

Like people, ferrets vary in what food they like. Some will go mad over a piece of fruit, others will turn up their noses at it. The same holds true for the ferret's interest in vegetables and cereal (cornflakes, shredded wheat, and so on). If your ferret enjoys any of these foods, fine. Just remember that they are supplements to its main diet of dried ferret food and should not be served in large quantities.

QUANTITY

Hard and fast rules cannot be laid down. The amount of food offered depends upon a number of factors such as the size of the ferret, its appetite, and how much exercise it has. Ferrets tend to eat less in warm weather and you need not worry about this. The general rule is that your pet should be given only what it can consume in five to ten minutes. A pregnant jill requires larger amounts than normal, and growing kits consume quite a lot of food.

VITAMINS AND MINERALS

There are various nutritional supplements on the market today. Caution is the key word here. If you are feeding your pet a varied, wholesome diet, no vitamin and mineral supplements are necessary. Of course, offering supplements to your pets is a good way to guard against dietary deficiencies. If you are concerned about your pet's diet, consult your veterinary surgeon or a reputable pet shop or breeder.

FEEDING ROUTINE

Wild polecats generally feed at dusk through to dawn, so offer the main meal to your pets in the evening and a lighter meal in the morning. It is best to work out a schedule and stick to it. The ferrets soon become accustomed to the routine and will await you eagerly at mealtime.

NO JUNK FOOD

Like other animals, ferrets can become overly fond of foods that are not good for them. Do not give your pets biscuits, chocolate or sweets, and avoid sticky items. Do not give them snack or junk food as it does them no good.

WATER

Ferrets drink quite a lot of water. You must put in a fresh supply every day and make sure it is available at all times. The drinking water can be put in a heavy, earthenware dish or, better yet, an automatic gravity-fed dispenser attached to the side of the cage. If you choose a dispenser, monitor the ferrets for a time so you know they can find the water.

FOOD DISHES

Probably the best food dishes are earthenware. They are easy to clean and heavy based which is important as otherwise they would be tipped over. Plastic dishes are too easily chewed and tossed around.

Breeding ferrets is very interesting but it is also a big responsibility. You must have the time, space and money to devote to a growing colony of ferrets. Before starting your breeding programme, you must know what you are going to do with the kits so find out what interest there is among friends and local pet shops.

No animal should be expected to reproduce unless it is in top condition. The birth process is very demanding on the jill. An unfit female is more likely to have problems during pregnancy and birth, and to produce small, weak young.

PHOTOINDUCTION

A ferret is induced into its sexual state by the length of the daylight hours. The male is light-negative, the female light-positive.

During the non-breeding season, the testes of the male recede into his body and are almost invisible under the heavy winter coat. About the time of the shortest day, his testicles begin to move back into the scrotum. He reaches his sexual peak about March or April. Depending upon the weather, he remains in a sexual state until the end of the summer. At this time, his testes begin to withdraw back into the body cavity.

The female comes into oestrus once the daylight hours begin to increase. She responds to a male when there are about 14 to 15 hours of daylight. Her litter is born, assuming an early mating, in May or June when the days are at their longest and warmest. A female responds to a male throughout the summer. She is in heat perpetually, not periodically, as are most other female animals. She is induced to ovulate only when stimulated by the presence of a male. Simply the scent of a male is enough to induce a jill to ovulate.

The kits are weaned at about eight weeks of age so they have the autumn to build up their supply of body fat for the coming winter. As the daylight hours shorten, the female goes out of oestrus and the breeding cycle is completed. An unmated female's oestrus ends by early autumn. If she is mated, she does not come into oestrus again until the young are reared.

With artificial light to extend daylight hours, it is possible to keep a captive ferret in breeding condition throughout the year. Experts advise against this method. Spring litters are far superior in strength to those produced during other periods.

Above: You can tell this is a true albino, because it has pink eyes.
Left: The 'robber's mask' over the eyes is characteristic of the wild polecat.

SEXING

Male ferrets are usually larger than females but the most obvious difference, of course, is the sex organs. The testes and anus are some distance apart in the male. The vulva and anus of the female are close together. The testes of the male are obvious in the breeding season. Likewise, the vulva of an unmated jill is dramatically enlarged in size during oestrus.

BREEDING AGE

Ferrets attain sexual maturity around six months of age. However, they should not be allowed to breed until they are one year old. Breeding less than fully mature stock results in inferior kits.

MATING

Once you are sure that both ferrets are ready to mate, introduce the jill to the male, never the other way round. The male will chase the female around his home. He will bite her on the neck behind the head and try to drag her to a sheltered position in order to mate with her. The female may escape a few times. If she is ready to be mated, though, eventually she will go limp. The hob will drag her to a convenient spot, throw her on her side and then mate. The whole process resembles a battle more than foreplay. The routine may be repeated over a few days after which you should separate the pair.

If the female is not ready to mate at this time, she will make the point clear to the male. Separate the pair and reintroduce them a few days later.

GESTATION AND BIRTH

The gestation period is about 42 days but this can vary a day or two either way. Increase the jill's food intake so that ample nourishment is passed to the growing embryos. The jill needs a dramatic increase in calcium so that her babies' bones grow properly, and to take her through the lactating period. Give her good-quality meat to help her produce vigorous youngsters.

As the birth draws near, the female starts to prepare a nest. Supply her with plenty of clean straw. She will also make use of dried leaves and wood shavings. Do not lift the female during her final stages of pregnancy. The first you should know of the actual birth is when you hear the squeaks of the newborn babies. A typical litter averages six to nine kits. They are born naked, blind and quite helpless.

REARING YOUNGSTERS

Avoid disturbing the nest for two weeks after the babies are born. The female is in a stressful state and the slightest concern for the welfare of her litter may result in her killing them. This is a natural instinct. She would rather do this than have them become a meal to a predator.

The vast majority of females are natural mothers and have no problems at all. Occasionally, a maiden ferret panics. She may ignore the babies, or even kill and eat them. This jill can be mated again but if the problem recurs, remove her from the breeding programme.

The newborns' pink skin is soon covered by white fur, which begins to darken in about seven days. The eyes of the kits open when they are about 21 days old. The babies soon start exploring the nest. They are very playful, having mock fights and attacking everything in their reach.

WEANING

By three weeks, the babies will be taking solid meat. They are weaned at about six to eight weeks of age. Give them bread and milk to ease the transition to solid food, and puppy meal mixed with finely chopped meat. They will be on an adult diet by the time they are ten weeks old. The ferret youngsters can be left together with the adults and will live as a small colony. At six months of age, though, it is wise to separate the sexes to prevent premature matings. Bear in mind that a jill mated early in the season may come into oestrus again. One litter per year is sufficient for any female.

PSEUDOPREGNANCY

Females who have ovulated may not have actually conceived. They may have a false pregnancy. This situation can occur when a female picks up the scent of a male, when she is mated to a sterile hob or simply when she is in the company of pregnant or nursing jills. The female develops as if she were actually pregnant. Her teats may swell and she may even produce milk and build a nest.

HAND-REARING

It may happen that a jill is an unfit mother, becomes ill or dies after giving birth. In such a case, it is wise to foster out her kits to other jills with young of their own. Wipe some of the foster mother's urine onto the abandoned kits. This lessens the chance of the new mother suspecting that the babies are not hers. You may not have another female with a litter of similar age but someone in your locality may have. This is where being a member of a club is really advantageous.

Sometimes it is necessary to hand-rear the kits. This is a tremendous undertaking as it entails bottle feeding the babies every two hours, 24 hours a day. If you opt to hand-feed, buy the smallest feeder bottle available; one made for kittens is about right. Feed the youngsters prepared milk for puppies. The milk should be given warm, but not hot.

The kits must be fed every two hours for about three weeks. Gradually cut the meals down to every three hours, then every four. You can offer human baby meat foods around 12 days of age. Introduce finely minced meat and chopped egg about the 15th day.

Above: This polecat ferret closely resembles its wild cousin.

Below: Ferrets do not like the water, but are skilful swimmers when they have to be.

Given adequate housing and a proper diet, a ferret will enjoy a life free of accidents and diseases. The greater the number of ferrets kept, the greater the risk of introducing and spreading infection. In addition, a ferret can pick up an infection from other animals. The key to good husbandry is prevention rather than cure. Examine your pets regularly and thoroughly for any signs of illness. Do not panic if you think your pet is off colour. Consult a veterinary surgeon about any problem that does not clear in 72 hours.

GENERAL CARE

Check the following aspects every week:

Teeth: A sloppy, soft-food diet results in food becoming lodged between the teeth which attracts bacteria. Likewise, small particles of bone can become embedded in the gums, creating ulcers and abscesses. Checking a ferret's teeth is a good idea for two reasons. First, the health of the teeth and gums can be ensured. Second, the ferret will get used to your opening its mouth, which is useful if you need to give it a pill or retrieve an item from its clench. You can clean a ferret's teeth with a canine toothpaste but this should not be necessary if you supply the correct diet.

Ears: Ferrets attract the same sort of ear parasites as dogs and cats. Scratching the ears is normal. Excessive scratching or carrying the head to one side is not. The external ear attracts a certain amount of debris which you can wipe away with a cotton swab soaked in a very mild antiseptic. Do not probe into the ear as overzealous cleaning can cause other problems. If any waxlike substance is visible deeper in the ear, consult your vet.

Nails: If exercised on hard ground, a ferret's nails will remain at a convenient length. The nails must be trimmed when they begin to curl and this is easily done with a pair of guillotine-type clippers used for dogs. Trim a little at a time. Be careful not to cut the 'quick', which is the blood vessel seen at the base of the nail. If you do cut the quick, stop the bleeding with a styptic pencil. If you are nervous about this procedure, let your vet do it rather than risk hurting the ferret.

Skin: Inspect the skin and fur for parasites and sores. Spikes of grass and straw can lodge in the skin. Any bald patches should be reported immediately to the vet.

Pads: Check the feet pads for any irritation. Again, this has the double advantage of being a health check and getting the ferret used to your holding its feet. Some ferrets enjoy having their pads gently rubbed.

VACCINATIONS

Ferrets are subject to most canine diseases but, fortunately, can be vaccinated against them. These diseases include distemper, leptospirosis, hepatitis (not canine), influenza, enteritis and botulism. The vaccinations are given around six to ten weeks of age and the ferret should have a booster injection each year. Discuss how many vaccinations your pet is given with your vet, who should be familiar with any diseases common in your area.

A group of coloured ferrets relaxing in the afternoon sun after a feed.

STERILISATION

Castration is the complete removal of a male's testes. This destroys his sexual drive and may also reduce the effect of the scent glands. A castrated hob exhibits much less aggression than normal during the breeding season and is less inclined to wander off. Given these advantages, it is probably better to sterilise any males purchased solely as pets. The procedure is usually done when the ferret is about six or seven months old. It is possible to remove a male's scent glands at the same time that he is castrated but this is not recommended, as it deprives the male of a vital defense mechanism against predators.

A male can also be made infertile by cutting the link between the testes and penis which prevents the sperm from passing through to the female. The male behaves normally in all other respects. He has the full drive and aggression of a typical male ferret.

A female kept purely as a pet is best spayed. This is a simple operation. The benefit is that all of the attendant risks of oestrus are removed.

PARASITES

A ferret can pick up all the external parasites which infect dogs, cats and rodents. Lice, mites and ticks live by sucking the blood of their hosts. If your dog or cat is being treated for these parasites, then your ferrets and their housing must be treated as well. Numerous treatments are available from pet shops. Dab ticks with petroleum jelly to make them release their hold.

ABSCESSES

Treat any swelling with concern. It may be only a localised reaction to an irritation, but it might be a tumour. A sudden reddish swelling is likely to be the result of an external cause, such as a bite or sting. Treat it with a mild antiseptic. Once a swelling has burst, swab it daily. Dust it with an appropriate powder to stop further infection of the wound.

Mouth abscesses are quite common in ferrets. Another area prone to abscess is the anus, especially in unmated jills. Prompt veterinary treatment is required.

The ferret has strong claws and paws, which help it to grip as it climbs.

DIARRHOEA

Normal ferret faeces are elongated, moist and firm. The faeces will become loose if sloppy or tainted foods are eaten. A stressed ferret will also have loose faeces.

Withdraw all food for 24 hours, which should solve the problem, but make sure that water is available at all times. If the faeces remain loose, foul-smelling or contain blood, a more serious condition is indicated. Diarrhoea is often a symptom of other ailments.

Isolate a ferret with persistent diarrhoea. Burn all its bedding material and disinfect the housing thoroughly. If you keep a number of ferrets, it is wise to have spare accommodation for situations such as this. Collect a sample of the faeces in a suitable container and take the sample and the ferret to the vet.

FLU AND CHILLS

A ferret can catch a cold from you or your other pets. Symptoms resemble those seen in humans - runny eyes and nose, high temperature, loss of appetite and drowsiness. Keep the ferret warm and away from stressful situations. Colds usually clear up quickly.

HEATSTROKE

Ferrets like to bask in the sun but can become overheated if they cannot retreat from the sunlight at their own convenience. Therefore a shaded area must be available to your pet. Never leave any animal in a closed car on a hot day.

A ferret suffering from heatstroke pants, becomes lethargic and needs immediate attention. Take it to a cool place and dip it in cool water. Do not use cold water, as too rapid a change in temperature may result in shock. Submerge the ferret's body, but be sure to hold its head above the water line. You can stroke the head with the cool water. Once the ferret appears to be reviving, towel it down and place it in a cool, dry spot. The area must be free from draughts so your pet does not get a chill.

SHOCK

The symptoms of shock resemble heatstroke. Shock can be caused by loud, sudden noise, being chased by a predator or by any similar, sudden movement. Be aware that the symptoms may not show immediately - there may be a delay from the time of the incident to the onset of shock.

Place an animal suffering from shock in a warm, quiet spot. Speak softly and gently stroke it. Recovery is normally rapid after some attention and a favoured titbit.

SUDDEN DEATH

Occasionally an animal dies quite suddenly without exhibiting any clinical signs of illness and in this case it is wise to have your vet conduct a post mortem to establish the cause of death. You need to know whether the cause was genetic, due to poor husbandry or was contagious in nature so that these factors can be corrected.

WOUNDS

Active, inquisitive ferrets often suffer minor wounds. All wounds should be carefully swabbed to establish their extent. Minor abrasions need little attention beyond cleansing with a mild antiseptic. More serious cuts must be cleaned. Put a dressing on the wound and take the ferret to a vet.

QUARANTINE

A period of quarantine is essential before introducing any new ferret to an established stock. Failure to do so is taking an unnecessary risk, regardless of how good the source of supply. Keep a new ferret isolated for a minimum of ten days to permit any incubating illness to show itself.

BIBLIOGRAPHY

FERRETS
Wendy Winsted, MD
ISBN 0-86622-829-2
KW-074

Introduction, Choosing Your Ferret, Handling, Feeding Your Ferret, Housebreaking, Ferret Grooming, Ferret Health, Ferret Reproductive Systems, Breeding and Birth, Ferret Play and Personality.

Hardcover: 142mm x 204mm, 128 pages, completely illustrated with full-colour photos and drawings.

FERRETS AS A NEW PET
Greg Ovechka
ISBN 0-86622-622-2
TU-014

Introduction, Handling Ferrets, Food for Ferrets, Bathing and Grooming, Housing, Health, Ferret Reproductive System, Ferrets and other Pets, Travelling with your Ferret, Colors, History

Softcover: 214 x 172mm, 64pp, 64 full-colour photographs

FERRETS IN YOUR HOME
Wendy Winsted, MD
ISBN 0-86622-988-4
TS-106
Contents: Introduction, Choosing Your Ferret, Temperament and Handling, Preparing for Arrival, Feeding Your Ferret, Housebreaking, Ferret Grooming, Ferret Health, Reproduction System, Breeding, Safety, Travelling with Your Ferret, Becoming a Two-Ferret Family, Ferrets and Other Animals, Ferret Lessons.

Hardcover: 142 x 204mm, 192 pages, over 90 full-colour photos and drawings.

A STEP-BY-STEP BOOK ABOUT FERRETS
Jay and Mary Field
ISBN 0-86622-462-9
SK-009

Introduction, Purchasing, Bringing Home, Playing and Handling, Ferret Curiosity, Health, Grooming, Breeding, Showing, Suggested Reading

Softcover: 214 x 136mm, 45 full colour photographs

The National Ferret Welfare Society
Tel: 01242 244520

will be happy to give you information about local clubs and activities.